Animal  Lives

CHEETAHS

Sally Morgan

QED Publishing

QED

First published in the UK in 2008 by
QED Publishing
A Quarto Group company
226 City Road
London EC1V 2TT

www.qed-publishing.co.uk

A Catalogue record for this book is
available from the British Library.

ISBN 978 1 84538 907 9

Written by Sally Morgan
Design and editorial by East River Partnership

Publisher Steve Evans
Creative Director Zeta Davies

Printed and bound in China

Picture Credits

Key: t = top, b = bottom, l = left, r = right,
c = centre, FC = front cover

Corbis /Winfried Wisniewski/zefa 5br, /Alan
& Sandy Carey /zefa 4–5, /Joe McDonald 23,
28–29 /Hulton-Deutsch Collection 27;
Ecoscene /Fritz Polking 8, /Fritz Polking 20,
/Sally Morgan 29; **Getty** /Anup Shah 11,
/Roger De La Harp 13, /Martin Harvey 15,
/Paul Souders 18; **NHPA** /Tom Ang 6, /Martin
Harvey 10–11, /Jonathan & Angela Scott 22;
Photolibrary /Joe McDonald 13, /Renee
Lynn 14–15; **The Print Collection** /Alamy 19;
Shutterstock /Willem Bosman 1, /Mark
Atkins 7, /Photobar 16bl, /Verena Ludemann
16–17, /Paul Vorwerk 17tr, /Steffen Foerster
Photography 19, /Keith Levit 20–21, /Sebastien
Burel 24–25, /Xtreme Safari Inc. 25t, /Steffen
Foerster Photography 30bl, /Mary Lane 30m,
/Chris Fourie 30tr.

Words in **bold** are explained
in the Glossary on page 31.

Contents

The cheetah

The cheetah is the fastest land animal in the world. It is a slim, long-legged big cat with a spotted coat. The cheetah's closest relatives are the other big cats, including the lion, tiger and leopard.

Hunters

Cheetahs are called **predators** because they hunt and eat other animals. Females usually live on their own, but male cheetahs either live on their own or as part of a small group with other males.

Type of mammal

The cheetah is a type of **mammal**. Mammals are animals that have hair on their body and give birth to live young. Female mammals also produce milk for their young. Other mammals include chimpanzees, dogs and zebras.

cheetah fact!

An adult cheetah weighs up to 65 kilograms and its body can grow to 135 centimetres long. Its tail is about 80 centimetres in length.

A cheetah's long legs allow it to bound over the ground at great speed.

Cheetahs are attractive animals, but they can be dangerous, too.

cheetah types

Most cheetahs have a golden-yellow coat that is covered with black spots. On their face, two black stripes run from the inside corner of their eyes to their mouth. These are called 'tear stripes'.

Different cheetahs

There is only one species, or type, of cheetah. But there are small differences between cheetahs living in different parts of the world. The desert cheetah of the Sahara, for example, has a much paler coat than most other cheetahs. This helps it to blend in with the colour of desert sand. Because of these differences, cheetahs are grouped into **subspecies**. There are three subspecies in Africa and two in Asia.

The Asiatic cheetah's coat is perfectly coloured for the grassland in which it lives.

Cheetah fact!

The word 'cheetah' comes from the Hindu word 'chita', which means 'the spotted one'.

Rare cheetah

The king cheetah is a rare type of cheetah that has large black blotches rather than spots on its coat. Fewer than 50 king cheetahs have been seen in the wild.

Most king cheetahs alive today, such as this one, have been bred in zoos and nature parks.

Where do you find cheetahs?

Cheetahs were once found right across Africa and the Middle East, and as far east as India. Today, most cheetahs live in Africa, to the south of the Sahara desert. Fewer than 100 cheetahs now live in Iran, in the Middle East. In recent years, only a few cheetahs have been seen in India and Pakistan.

This cheetah has climbed on to a tree trunk to get a better view over the savannah.

cheetah fact!

In the 19th century, explorers thought that they had discovered 'woolly' cheetahs. But these were just normal cheetahs with extra-long fur.

Cheetah habitats

Cheetahs like to live in open grassland where they have plenty of space to run and hunt. That is why the African **savannah** – a huge, flat grassland with only a few trees – is a perfect place. Rocky outcrops in the savannah make ideal spots for the cheetahs to sit quietly and watch for **prey** and predators. A few cheetahs also live on very dry grasslands near deserts or in colder mountainous areas.

EUROPE

ASIA

AFRICA

INDIAN OCEAN

ATLANTIC OCEAN

Parts of Africa and Asia where cheetahs live.

9

Beginning life

Once a female cheetah has mated with a male cheetah, she will be **pregnant** for about three months before giving birth to her **litter** of cubs.

Newborn cubs

When they are born, cheetah cubs are helpless and cannot walk. They weigh just 350 grams, less than a small bag of sugar, and are about 30 centimetres long from the tip of their nose to the top of their tail. Although cheetah cubs are born with their eyes shut, they start to feed on their mother's milk immediately. A cheetah cub's eyes will open when it is five to eleven days old.

cheetah fact!

Most female cheetahs give birth to a litter of between three and five cubs. Sometimes, females have as many as eight cubs.

Cheetah cubs have grey hair and a mane of long hair down their back.

Avoiding danger

The cheetah mother looks after the cubs on her own. This means that when she goes hunting for food, she has to leave her cubs by themselves. To avoid danger from predators, such as lions and hyenas, the mother hides the cubs in a safe place where they will not be found. To be extra safe, she moves the cubs every few days to a new hiding place. As the cubs cannot walk until they are about 16 days old, the mother has to carry them, one by one. She picks them up by gently biting the skin on the back of their necks.

These cubs are suckling milk from their mother.

11

Growing up

For the first 12 weeks after they are born, the cheetah mother feeds the cubs her own milk. The cubs' first teeth begin to appear when they are three weeks old. By the time they are six weeks old, the cubs are able to follow their mother and begin to eat meat.

Playing helps cheetah cubs to practise their hunting and fighting skills.

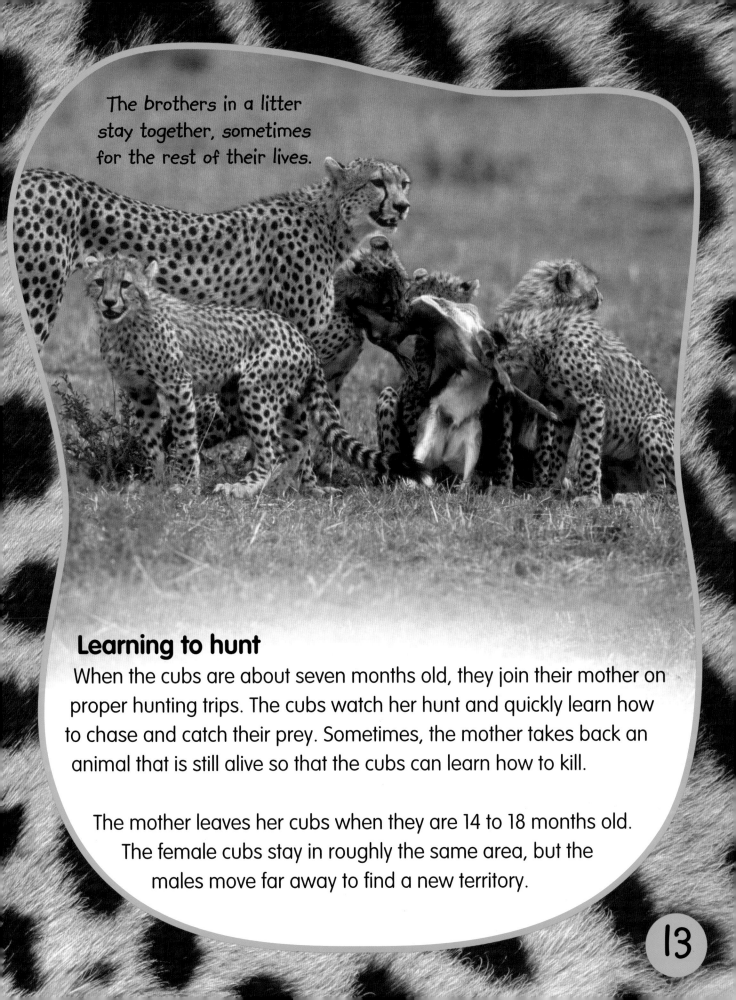

The brothers in a litter stay together, sometimes for the rest of their lives.

Learning to hunt

When the cubs are about seven months old, they join their mother on proper hunting trips. The cubs watch her hunt and quickly learn how to chase and catch their prey. Sometimes, the mother takes back an animal that is still alive so that the cubs can learn how to kill.

The mother leaves her cubs when they are 14 to 18 months old. The female cubs stay in roughly the same area, but the males move far away to find a new territory.

Cheetah movement

Although an adult cheetah can reach an amazing top speed of about 100 kilometres an hour when it needs to, it usually runs at a slower 60 to 70 kilometres an hour when chasing after its prey.

Built for speed

The cheetah's slim body, long legs and bendy back are built for speed. It can take long strides and move across the ground quickly. Large lungs allow the cheetah to breathe plenty of air, and a long tail helps it to keep its balance, especially when changing direction.

The cheetah gets very hot when running fast, so it can only run at top speed for about one minute. After this, the cheetah has to stop or its body will get too hot.

A cheetah's powerful tail helps it to stay balanced when turning.

Firm grip

The cheetah's claws are never completely **retracted**. They help it keep a firm grip on the ground when running.

These cheetahs are seen at full stretch as they lift all four legs off the ground while running fast.

cheetah fact!

A cheetah can run 100 metres in less than four seconds. This is over twice as fast as any human is able to run.

carnivores

Cheetahs are **carnivores**, or meat eaters, and need to eat as much as 3 kilograms of meat every day. They usually hunt animals such as deer, antelopes and hares, although sometimes they will also catch warthogs and birds. As cheetahs get plenty of water from the food they eat, they only drink fresh water every few days.

Cheetah teeth

A cheetah has extra-large nostrils so that it can breathe in lots of air when running fast. This leaves less room for its jaws and teeth, which are smaller than those in other big cats. A cheetah slices through its food using its back teeth and then swallows it in large chunks. It has a very rough tongue, which it uses to scrape bits of meat from the bone. Unlike the hyena, a cheetah cannot crush bones.

A cheetah uses its long, pointed teeth to grip its prey firmly.

Quick eaters

After it has killed its prey, a cheetah will drag it away and eat it quickly. A cheetah does this because bigger predators, such as lions and hyenas, will chase the cheetah away and steal its kill if they see it with food on the ground.

When they hunt together, a family of cheetahs can bring down and kill large prey, such as this water buck.

Cheetahs kill their prey and then drag it under cover before eating it.

cheetah fact!

It takes a cheetah about three years to become a fully skilled hunter.

Hunting

Cheetahs hunt during the day when larger predators, such as lions, are sleeping. When hunting alone, its prey has to be small enough for a cheetah to bring down and kill on its own.

Closer and closer

A cheetah hunts by slowly stalking its prey, sometimes for many hours at a time. It creeps closer and closer until it is ready to attack. The cheetah's spotted coat helps it to move in long grass without being seen.

This cheetah family is bringing down a Thomson's gazelle.

Changing direction

When it is close to its prey, a cheetah leaps up and gives chase at high speed for about 20 to 30 seconds. Although cheetahs can run extremely fast in a straight line, they have to slow down when changing direction. This is why prey animals usually zigzag when fleeing.

This cheetah has killed its prey by biting through its neck.

Knocked to the ground

When it is close enough, a cheetah knocks over its prey with a swipe from a front paw and pounces on it. If the animal is small, the cheetah will kill it by biting through its neck. To kill larger prey, the cheetah clamps its jaws tightly around the animal's neck so that it **suffocates**.

Cheetah senses

Cheetahs use their senses of smell, hearing and, most importantly, sight to find their prey when hunting.

Eyes for hunting

A cheetah's excellent eyesight allows it to see its prey from far away. Because its eyes face forward, a cheetah can tell how far away an animal is and how far it has to run. A cheetah's eyes also have what is known as a 'wide angle of view'. This means that when it looks straight ahead, a cheetah can see to the sides at the same time. This is ideal for hunting on the wide, flat grasslands on which most cheetahs live. If an animal moves in the distance, the cheetah will see it!

From behind, a cheetah's ears look like eyes. Predators may think it can see them and not attack.

Listening for prey

The cheetah has small, round ears that it uses to listen out for rustling noises made by even its smallest prey. All cheetahs, especially mothers with cubs, also carefully listen for the approach of dangerous predators, such as lions and hyenas.

Cheetahs have a large nose but their sense of smell is not as important as their sense of sight.

cheetah fact!

The tear stripes on the cheetah's face may help to reduce the sun's glare. Some sportsmen put black make-up under their eyes for the same reason.

Living in a territory

Cheetahs live in an area called a **territory**, where they find their food and water. Normally, cheetahs never leave their territory.

Size of territory

Territories are not always the same size. Where there is plenty of food, for example, the territory can be small. In desert areas, where food and water are scarce, a territory can be as large as 1000 square kilometres. This is the size of a big city.

Male cheetahs can hurt each other badly when they fight to defend their territory.

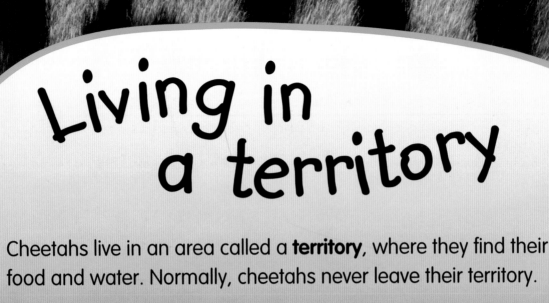

Guarding a territory

When cheetah brothers move away from their mother to find their own territory, they usually stay together. Sometimes, they are joined by young males from other families. Once a male group has found a new territory, it will protect it by marking boulders and termite mounds with strong-smelling **urine** to warn other males to stay away. Male cheetahs will fight, and even kill, other males that enter their territory.

Close to mother

Unlike male cheetahs, females do not guard their territory. Female cheetahs usually stay in the same area as their mothers, and may share parts of her territory.

This male cheetah is marking a tree at the edge of its territory.

cheetah talk

Cheetahs make many sounds to communicate with each other when resting and hunting. But cheetahs cannot roar like lions, because the bones in their throats are hard and closer together.

When two adult cheetahs meet, they greet each other by making a soft 'churring' sound.

24

This little cub is waiting for its mother to return from a hunting trip.

Purring and growling

When it is happy and relaxed, a cheetah will purr gently like a domestic cat. Unlike a domestic cat, however, which can purr continuously, a cheetah only purrs when breathing out. When it is threatened, a cheetah can growl like a dog as a warning.

Keeping in touch

When her cubs have wandered off, a female cheetah makes a distinctive, high-pitched bark as a signal for them to return to her. When the cubs want to attract their mother, however, they make a shrill, chirping sound. A cheetah mother can hear her cubs chirping from as far away as one kilometre.

cheetah fact!

A cheetah can make a high-pitched chirping that sounds just like a bird call. Birds hear this and fly down. Then the cheetah catches them!

cheetahs and people

In the past, cheetahs were sometimes kept as pets or to take on hunting expeditions. This does not happen any more as we now prefer to see cheetahs living free in their natural **habitat**.

Hunting with a cheetah

Cheetahs were first tamed and used for hunting about 5000 years ago by the Sumerians, a people who lived in the Middle East. Later on, Arab and Indian princes kept cheetahs for hunting. During a hunt, a cheetah would be released from its cage to run and catch prey after the prey had been found by hunting dogs.

The Ancient Egyptians sometimes took their pet cheetahs on hunting expeditions.

Egyptian pharaohs

Records show that the pharaohs of Ancient Egypt kept cheetahs as pets. A cheetah was considered to be extremely valuable, and many paintings and statues of cheetahs have been discovered in Ancient Egyptian sites.

The American entertainer Josephine Baker had a pet cheetah called Chiquita that wore a diamond collar.

cheetah fact!

Emperor Akbar the Great of India, who ruled between 1555 and 1600, owned about 1000 cheetahs. Sadly, only one litter of cubs was born during the many years that he kept cheetahs.

Cheetahs under threat

One hundred years ago, over 100 000 cheetahs could be found living in the wild. Today, there are fewer than 12 000, making the cheetah an **endangered** animal that is at risk of becoming **extinct**.

Loss of habitats

In the past, many cheetahs were hunted for their fur, which was used to make expensive coats. Cheetahs were also killed by farmers, who wanted to protect their **livestock**. Today, the main threat to the cheetah comes from the loss of its habitat – the place where it lives. This is especially the case with grasslands. More and more, these grasslands are being used to graze cattle and sheep and to grow crops.

cheetah fact!

The majority of cheetahs are now found in Africa, especially in Namibia in south-west Africa.

Watching a cheetah is often the highlight of a safari holiday in Africa.

Saving cheetahs

Fortunately, people are making a big effort to save the cheetah. Animals are now being protected in national parks where hunting and grazing is banned. Instead, tourists are invited to watch cheetahs. Their visits bring money into an area, which encourages local people to look after the cheetahs.

Life cycle of a cheetah

Cub

Juvenile

Adult

A female cheetah is ready to breed when she is about two years old. She gives birth to between three and five cubs. The cubs stay with her for up to 18 months. A cheetah lives for between five and twelve years in the wild but up to 17 years in a zoo.

Glossary

carnivore an animal that hunts and eats other animals

endangered animals that may become extinct if something is not done to protect them

extinct animals or plants that have died out completely

habitat the place in which an animal or plant lives

litter two or more young animals born together, to one mother

livestock farm animals, such as cows, pigs and chickens

mammal an animal that gives birth to live young, rather than laying eggs. Female mammals produce milk to feed their young

predator an animal that hunts other animals

pregnant a female animal that has a baby, or babies, developing inside her

prey an animal that is hunted by other animals

retracted pulled in, as a cat can pull in its claws

savannah grassland in a hot country

subspecies groups within a species that look slightly different from each other

suffocate to die because breathing is prevented

territory an area in which an animal spends its life and where it finds all its food and water

urine waste liquid that is passed out of the body

Index